Substance Abuse and Cognitive Behavioral Therapy

Toward the Development of a Substance Abuse Treatment Program

Based on

Cognitive Behavioral Therapy and Self-Efficacy Theory

With A Focus On Self-Evaluation and

Self-Cognition

Substance Abuse and Cognitive Behavioral Therapy

Dr. Roham Ghassemi

To order additional copies of this book, contact:
Xlibris
844-714-8691
www.Xlibris.com
Orders@Xlibris.com
847599

CONTENTS

Substance Abuse and Cognitive Behavioral Therapy

Theory and research suggest that self-efficacy plays an important part in substance abusers' decisions to change substance-related behavior, reduce substance use during treatment, and maintain treatment progress at follow-up. Self-evaluation and self-cognition can help individuals develop the self-efficacy to overcome substance abuse and make better life choices.

The purpose of this investigation was to examine the current literature on substance abuse treatments, cognitive behavioral theory (CBT), self-efficacy theory, self-evaluation, and self-cognition strategies to identify components of the above that are empirically important and might logically be included in a substance abuse treatment program. Through a critical analysis of existing theory related to CBT and self-efficacy, the components that might be included in an intervention to reduce substance abuse were identified.

The goal of the intervention would be to reduce substance abuse by helping participants become more aware of their feelings and reactions and changing them in ways that will support cessation of substance abuse. A twelve-session, six-week program for individuals ranging in age from twenty-five to fifty was developed. Components of the intervention include helping clients capture thoughts, feelings, and sensations; identify and label feelings; identify positive and negative expectancies of substance abuse; demonstrate awareness of triggers for substance abuse; seek out alternative interpretations of substance abuse thoughts and behaviors; and modify existing cognitive structures.

Chapter One

Introduction

Background of the Problem

The treatment of substance abuse and substance dependence has an extensive history and includes biological, psychological, and sociological components. The DSM-IV-TR (APA 2000) defines *substance abuse* as the "maladaptive pattern of substance use manifested by recurrent and significant adverse consequences related to the repeated use of substance. The substance-related problem must have occurred repeatedly during the same twelve-month period or been persistent" (p. 128). *Substance dependence* is "a cluster of cognitive, behavioral, and physiological symptoms indicating that the individual continues use of the substance despite significant substance-related problems" (p. 192).

The DSM-IV-TR (APA 2000) criteria for substance abuse are the following:

1. Recurrent substance use that results in the person not fulfilling major obligations at work, school, or home
2. Recurrent substance use in physically hazardous situations

3. Recurrent substance-related legal problems
4. Continued substance use despite persistent or recurrent social or interpersonal problems caused or aggravated by the effects of the substance (APA 2000)

The DSM-IV-TR (APA 2000) lists the following criteria for substance dependence:

1. Tolerance, which is indicated by the need for a significantly increased amount of the substance to achieve the desired effect or a significantly diminished effect with continued use of the same amount of the substance
2. Withdrawal symptoms (as outlined in Criteria *A* and *B* of withdrawal criteria) or use of the substance to relieve or avoid withdrawal symptoms
3. Taking greater amounts of the substance or using the substance over a longer period of time than intended
4. A persistent desire or unsuccessful attempts to cut down or control substance use
5. Spending much time on activities related to obtaining and using the substance or recovering from its effects
6. Giving up or reducing important social, occupational, or recreational activities because of substance use
7. Continuing the use of the substance despite knowing about its persistent negative physiological or psychological effects

A diagnosis of substance dependence is rendered when the person meets a minimum of three out of these seven criteria within a twelve-month period.

The disease model of addiction proposes that substance misuse is caused by a fundamental biological or psychological susceptibility that results in an individual's loss of control of consumption of the misused substance (Ouimette, Finney, and Moos 1997). This conceptualization posits that persons are powerless to control their problematic behaviors and are unable to refrain from substance abuse by themselves, just as persons with a terminal illness cannot fight their disease without medication (Futterman, Lorente, and Silverman 2005).

The medical frame of reference thus supports the disease model that is used in some addiction intervention or prevention treatment approaches. This approach involves educating abusers and their families about the genetic origins of the disease and encouraging abstinence from the substance (Ouimette et al. 1997). Conventional twelve-step models, which are based on a self-help orientation, combine the components of the Alcoholics Anonymous program with the disease model of addiction (Ouimette et al. 1997). Persons who participate in the twelve-step treatment are instructed to accept the disease model of substance abuse, identify themselves as alcoholics or addicts, and assume the goal of abstinence. In addition, they are taught to participate in the twelve-step process, which includes attending twelve-step meetings, obtaining a sponsor, and following the recommended steps (Ouimette et al. 1997).

Some researchers (Ball 2007; Futterman et al. 2005; Matto 2007) questioned the validity of the diseased person model of substance abuse treatment, arguing that this model exacerbates abusers' feeling of powerlessness and worthlessness, and that individuals are capable of changing their behaviors.

Several theories and approaches were introduced that attempt to explain behavior change.

Rogers (1959) developed the client-centered approach to therapy, in which the therapist shows genuineness, empathy, and unconditional positive regard toward a client to create a supportive, nonjudgmental environment in which the clients are encouraged to reach their full potential. Rogers proposed that personal change takes place when three conditions are present: unconditional positive regard, accurate empathy, and genuineness. Within the therapeutic relationship, Rogers believed the existence of these three conditions could help clients overcome any troubling issues, including alcohol abuse.

Psychoanalytic approaches to behavior change have also explained substance abuse. Freud (1955, 1957) suggested that the main cause of substance abuse and dependence is the person's unconscious need to entertain and to enact various kinds of homosexual and perverse fantasies by the use of certain drugs. Substance abuse is viewed as associated with traumatic life experiences brought about by social, cultural, and political factors; fantasizing while using certain substances are viewed as the person's way of coping with trauma (Hopper 1995).

Psychoanalytic approaches contrast with cognitive theories and approaches, which posit that persons are able to regulate and control their physical and cognitive environments rather than simply being driven by or responding to impulses. In addition, homosexuality is not a key component of substance abuse (Drescher 2008; Rotgers Morgenstern, and Walters 2006).

Marlatt and Gordon (1985) introduced the concept of using cognitive-behavioral strategies in treating substance abuse. As it relates to substance abuse treatment, the underlying assumption of CBT is relapse that can be controlled by developing new cognitive, emotional, and behavioral choices (Matto 2007).

Bandura (1986, 1997) conceptualized self-efficacy as a person's beliefs in his or her competence to successfully perform a given task or behavior and reach specific goals. For substance abusers, self-efficacy to maintain abstinence and avoid relapse has been shown to play an important role in changing substance-related behavior, reducing substance use during treatment, and maintaining treatment progress (Benda 2002; Levin, Ilgen, and Moos 2007; Nes and Oei 2005). However, self-efficacy might be differentially related to treatment outcomes depending on the individual's level of self-cognition and self-evaluation.

The use of CBT to treat substance abuse has substantial empirical support (Carroll 1996, 1998; Carroll, Rounsaville, Gordon, et al. 1994; Carroll, Rounsaville, Nich, et al. 1994; Marlatt 1985). For instance, Carroll, Rounsaville, Gordon, et al. (1994) and Carroll, Rounsaville, Nich, et al. (1994) studied the efficacy of cognitive behavioral therapy (CBT) for the treatment of cocaine dependence and found that the use of CBT reduced cocaine use over a one-year period. These and other studies provide empirical support for use of CBT in treating cocaine dependence (Aharonovich et al. 2008; Carroll 1998; Rawson et al. 1995; Shoptaw et al. 1994) and for usefulness of using CBT to treat methamphetamine users (Huber et al. 1997; Rawson et al. 2000; Shoptaw et al. 2005).

The integration of formerly disjointed psychological approaches has resulted in major developments in the theory and technique of substance abuse treatment. Theories emerging from the coming together of the two fields include the theory of harm reduction (Marlatt 1998), as it relates to substance abuse, the techniques of relapse prevention (Marlatt and Gordon 1985), and the technique of motivational interviewing (Miller and Rollnick 2002).

Harm reduction includes a set of practical strategies, ranging from safer use to abstinence, to reduce the negative consequences of substance use, incorporating a spectrum of strategies from safer use to abstinence (Futterman et al. 2005). Futterman et al. proposed a harm reduction model of substance abuse treatment that integrates recent emphasis on behavioral, cognitive-behavioral, and psychodynamic techniques, and works on the process of behaviors in session.

Relapse prevention focuses more on maintaining behavior changes relative to substance abuse and teaching the individual to effectively anticipate and cope with potential relapse situations (Marlatt 1985).

Motivational interviewing is a set of techniques and approaches toward clients where the therapist assumes that clients are usually ambivalent about their use of substances. The therapist does not advocate the use or nonuse of drugs, but encourages clients to weigh their own arguments for and against the use of drugs (Miller and Rollnick).

The relapse prevention treatment model (Marlatt and Gordon 1985) is one of the most widely used CBT models in treating substance abuse (Ball 2007). According to Marlatt (1985), there are four psychosocial processes related to the addiction and relapse processes: self-efficacy, outcome expectancies, attributions of causality, and decision-making processes. With respect to relapse situations, *self-efficacy* refers to one's ability to deal competently and effectively with situations that carry a high risk of relapse. *Outcome expectancies* refer to a person's expectations about the effects of an addictive substance (i.e., changes in mood, perceptions, or behavior). *Attributions of causality* refer to a person's beliefs about whether relapse is the result of internal or external causes. Substance use is the result of multiple decisions about using the substance and that may place the user at risk for relapse.

Marlatt and Gordon's (1985) model originally extended Bandura's (1986, 1997) theory, which proposed that self-efficacy, in terms of addictive behavior, was a function of the interrelationship between environmental factors (e.g., drug availability, peers, etc.)

and psychological factors (e.g., cognition, affect, coping, etc.) that determine whether relapse will occur. Thus, this model emphasizes that cognitive interpretations and behavioral reactions to environmental events are relevant to the origins of substance abuse, maintaining addiction, and type of treatment intervention. An updated relapse prevention model (Witkiewitz and Marlatt 2004) proposed that low self-efficacy makes individuals vulnerable to relapse, which may be aggravated by poor coping skills.

Beck et al. (2001) described a cognitively based model of substance abuse recovery based on Beck's (1975) model of cognitive therapy, which posited that the way persons feel and behave depends on how they interpret their experiences. Psychological disorders come about when persons' beliefs are dysfunctional. Beliefs are relatively stable cognitive processes that are not easily modified by experience. These beliefs may lead to dysfunctional thinking and improvement results from modifying these dysfunctional beliefs and thoughts (Beck 1975).

As applied to substance abuse, there are three categories of dysfunctional beliefs associated with a person's decision to abuse substances: anticipatory, relief-oriented, and facilitative or permissive (Beck et al. 2001).

Cognitive therapy assumes that persons who abuse substances have core beliefs that are often unconscious, such as "When I use, I am invincible." These result in imagined anticipatory benefits of substance use and a craving for the substance or substances. The activation of the craving leads to relief-oriented beliefs: "I need this to make the cravings go away." Permissive beliefs (e.g., "I deserve this") attempt to justify use of the substance.

The objective of cognitive therapy is to uncover the person's underlying belief system, analyze it with the person, and modify the dysfunctional beliefs, or cognitive distortions, with cognitive restructuring, or replace faculty beliefs with more functional beliefs (Beck et al. 2001). For example, Shoal and Giancola (2005) examined the relationship between social problems and adolescent substance use in the context of several variables—one of which was cognitive distortion. Shoal and Giancola found that persons with low levels of cognitive distortion are more likely to choose more adaptive methods of coping with social problems and reduce the potential risk of drug use. Persons with high levels of cognitive distortions resulting from faulty beliefs and misperceptions are at increased risk for social difficulties and for behaviors such as substance use and abuse.

Witkiewitz and Marlatt (2007) cited two empirical studies of the efficacy of cognitive behavioral therapy that taught both high-risk and low-risk adolescents coping skills. Azrin et al. (2001, as cited in Witkiewitz and Marlatt) found that six months of cognitive therapy among fifty-six adolescents resulted in a decrease in substance abuse. Dennis et al. (2004, as cited in Witkiewitz and Marlatt) studied youths aged twelve to eighteen years who used marijuana and found increased days of abstinence from marijuana over a twelve-month period. Witkiewitz and Marlatt concluded that cognitive therapy alone or in combination with other methods is a promising treatment for relapse prevention.

Miller and Carpenter (2005) outlined the elements of behavioral treatment of substance abuse. Treatment begins with a functional analysis of behavior to determine the reasons people use and abuse drugs and to build the foundation for treatment. The assessment includes determining where, when, how much, and with whom the person uses the substance; triggers of use; consequences or reinforcers of use; and the person's expected and desired effects of the use. In addition to assessing substance use, the functional analysis examines the skills, strengths, and motivation for change. Persons are also instructed to self-evaluate their addictive behaviors.

After the functional analysis is complete, treatment includes specific skill development, such as coping skills, refusal skills, managing urges and cravings, and a discussion of seemingly irrelevant decisions (SIDS), which are small choices, but when taken together facilitate drug use. Treatment goals include recognizing, avoiding, and coping with these seemingly irrelevant decisions. Cognitive behavioral treatment also incorporates life skills training in such skills as managing negative thinking, promoting self-efficacy, anger management, receiving criticism, nonverbal communication, assertiveness, conversation skills, giving or receiving positive feedback, listening skills, constructive criticism, resolving relationship problems, developing social supports, problem solving, and increasing pleasant activities (Miller and Carpenter, 2005).

Practitioners who work with substance abusers recognize the physiological and genetic aspects of substance use; however, they also operate under the theoretical assumption that addiction is a learned behavior and that treatment techniques based on self-evaluation and self-cognition can be used to change behavior (McCusker 2001; Robinson et al. 2006). Thus, medication and behavioral therapy, alone or in combination, are aspects of an overall therapeutic approach.

Behavioral interventions for drug and alcohol dependence have been tested in several controlled clinical trials (e.g., Robinson et al. 2006), and self-evaluation and self-cognition have been shown to contribute to an accurate functional analysis of behavior and eventual recovery (Litt et al. 2008). Despite evidence from the research, many people who struggle with substance abuse are not successful in initially abstaining from substance abuse; some may experience initial success, only to relapse.

For this reason, treatment should focus on relapse prevention (Miller and Carpenter 2005). Cognitions related to "falling off the wagon" or temporary episodes of use are discussed from the vantage point of the abstinence violation effect (AVE), a common cognitive phenomenon in which a lapse is viewed as a total relapse. The abstinent individual who lapses once may develop the perception that one lapse makes abstinence impossible, which leads to further lapses. Relapse prevention treatment teaches the person to challenge these notions with new and more positive cognitive statements (Miller and Carpenter).

Statement of the Problem

It is important that individuals know the source of their behaviors and why they behave a certain way if they are to have higher levels of self-efficacy. CBT helps abusers recognize and cope with their addictive behavior. For substance users and abusers, self-efficacy plays an important part in making decisions to change substance-related behavior, reducing substance use during treatment, and maintaining treatment progress at follow-up (Benda 2002; Dolan et al. 2008; Kranz and O'Hare 2006; Levin et al. 2007; McKellar et al. 2008; McLellan 2008;

Self-evaluation and self-cognition can help individuals develop the self-efficacy to overcome substance abuse and make better life choices. Therefore, the proposed research addressed the following research question: Based on current research and theory, what components of CBT and self-efficacy theory might logically be included in a treatment program that focuses on reducing substance abuse using self-cognition and self-evaluation methods?

Purpose of the Study

The purpose of this research was to examine the current literature on substance abuse treatments, CBT, self-efficacy theory, self-evaluation, and self-cognition strategies to identify components of the above that are empirically important and might logically be included in a substance abuse treatment program. There is ample literature that shows that the more an individual engages in treatment, the greater the prospects for successful outcomes.

Self-evaluation and self-cognition are important elements in engagement in treatment. In addition, the literature is clear that no single treatment is effective for all individuals. Therefore, treatment approaches, particularly those involving self-evaluation and self-cognition methods, were explored via an extensive review of the current literature to identify components that have been empirically supported and might logically be included in a substance abuse treatment program.

Definitions of Terms

Addiction: A chronic relapsing condition characterized by dependence on and use of drugs such as alcohol, amphetamines, cocaine, heroin, marijuana, or nicotine (McLellan 2008).

Cognitive behavioral therapy (CBT): Short-term psychotherapy based on the concept that one's cognitive thoughts affect emotions and feelings. CBT is a problem-solving approach that focuses on present thinking, behavior, and communication rather than on past experiences (Rosenblum et al. 2005). As applied to substance abuse, CBT is used to control relapse by developing new cognitive and emotional choices that are manifested in behavioral choices (Matto 2007).

Self-concept: An individual's knowledge about the self, including beliefs regarding personality traits, physical characteristics, abilities, values, goals, and roles (Kaplan 2008).

Self-cognition: A construct that is part of the self-concept, whereby the individual defines the nature and qualities of the self (including perception, conception, and awareness) but without evaluation (Kaplan 2008).

Self-efficacy: "People's judgments of their capabilities to organize and execute courses of action required to attain designated types of performance" (Bandura 1986, 391).

Self-evaluation: How clients felt about themselves or how they believe others feel about them (Robinson et al. 2006). One's ability to self-evaluate is a function of his or her self-concept and self-cognition (Kaplan 2008).

Substance abuse: The excessive use of drugs, such as alcohol, amphetamines, cocaine, heroin, marijuana, or nicotine (McLellan 2008).

Limitations of the Study

It was anticipated that the proposed substance abuse treatment program may be used in a variety of settings and with varied individuals. However, the wide application of the program may have limitations. First, conclusions about substance abuse and substance dependence and treatment programs were limited by the amount of relevant data available in books, documents, reports, and databases. The results of this critical analysis of the literature may not generalize to all substance abusers; rather, generalizability may be limited to specific populations (e.g., adolescents, older individuals, etc.) or types of substance abuse (e.g., alcohol, cocaine, methamphetamine, etc.) that are studied in the literature. For example, if the majority of the research has been conducted on adolescents, the researcher can only generalize to adolescents. Therefore, the researcher reviewed a wide range of the literature to ensure greater generalizability to a greater population.

Chapter Two

Theoretical Foundations of Substance Abuse Treatment

Introduction and Overview

In the previous chapter, the background of the problem of the present research, the problem statement, and purpose and limitations of the study were presented. In addition, terms that will be unique in the study were operationally defined.

In this study, the components of cognitive behavioral therapy (CBT) and self-efficacy theory might logically be included in an examination of the current literature on substance abuse treatments to identify their empirical relevance and potential inclusion in a substance abuse treatment program. In this chapter, CBT and self-efficacy as related to the treatment of substance abuse is discussed in more detail.

Cognitive Behavioral Therapy

Cognitive behavioral therapy (CBT) is based on a combination of behavioral theory and cognitive theory (Carroll and Onkin 2005). Cognitive theory posits that most psychological problems derive from a faulty thinking process (Beck, Liese, and Najavits 2005).

CBT is similar to cognitive therapy because it emphasizes analyzing the current problematic situation of substance abusers and their thoughts and reactions associated with substance abuse (Beck et al. 2005).

CBT differs from cognitive therapy because the primary focus of treatment is identifying, understanding, and changing substance abusers' underlying beliefs about themselves in relationship to substance abuse (Beck et al. 2005).

SAMSHA (2003) defined CBT as an approach that "helps people change negative thought patterns, beliefs, and behaviors so they can manage symptoms and enjoy more productive, less stressful lives" (p. 5). Individuals are taught to realistically appraise their experiences by monitoring and changing distorted thinking. Thus, CBT takes cognitive therapy one step further by not only attempting to change substance abusers' thinking but also their coping behaviors.

Attribution, appraisals, self-efficacy, and expectancies are elements of cognitive theory included in cognitive-behavioral therapy. An attribution is an individual's explanation of why an event occurred and is at the heart of CBT for substance abuse disorders (Marlatt 1996).

Some individuals may attribute events and their causes to internal forces; for example, a cocaine user may say he or she was weak—an internal attribute. Others may attribute events and causes to external forces; for example, an individual may say that he or she succumbed to peer pressure to use cocaine.

Attributional style is believed to influence whether individuals believe they have a substance abuse problem and whether they can overcome the problem.

Cognitive appraisal is the extent to which individuals appraises a situation as stressful and their ability to cope with the situation (McCusker 2001). Cognitive appraisal is viewed as a necessary adjunct to the individual's coping skills and coping strategies.

Self-efficacy, which will be discussed in more detail in this chapter, refers to individuals' confidence in their ability to resist using substances. Individuals with higher levels of self-efficacy are less likely to abuse substances, while those with lower levels of self-efficacy are more likely to abuse substances (Levin et al. 2007).

Expectancies, as they relate to substance abuse, are individuals' expectations that substance abuse will produce either positive or negative certain effects (Marlatt 1985). Examples of positive effects are euphoria, relaxation, and sexual enhancement. Examples of negative effects are aggression, careless risk taking, anxiety, or depression.

The objective of CBT for substance abuse is to modify thoughts associated with substance abuse and to develop new behaviors to replace dysfunctional behaviors (Beck et al. 2005). While therapists may delve into issues in the past that relate to clients' beliefs and addictive behavior, CBT is focused on present problems (Beck et al. 2005).

In CBT for substance abuse, individuals must identify situations that may prompt them to abuse substances and learn new coping skills to help them resist such situations. Among the instructional techniques used are modeling, role-plays, and rehearsals. Relaxation training and stress-reduction methods help clients realize that they can relieve some of the pressures that confront them without abusing substances may also be included (Otto, O'Cleirigh, and Pollack, 2007).

Another key objective of CBT is relapse prevention. Relapse prevention approaches involve identifying high-risk relapse situations and providing appropriate coping skills training that target the cognitions involved in the relapse process and help individuals gain more positive self-efficacy beliefs (Marlatt 1985). CBT relapse prevention also challenges the client's positive self-expectancies about the effects of using alcohol or drugs, either by changing the client's beliefs about the positive effects of using the substance or by drawing the client's attention to the negative effects (Ball 2007).

CBT also emphasizes that relapse is possible and that steps must be taken to avoid the relapse or to prepare for it. Relapse avoidance strategies include promoting a balanced and health lifestyle that helps individuals make better decisions and, in turn, prevent relapse and high-risk behavior. Role-plays and candidly assessing the possibility of relapse are important. Including family members in relapse planning is also important, as often the family will see the behaviors that lead to relapse that the substance abuser does not see or refuses to see (Miller and Carpenter 2005).

Self-Efficacy

The concept of self-efficacy is an outgrowth of social cognitive theory and, as proposed by Bandura (1986, 1997), is the extent to which individuals perceive themselves as capable of performing certain tasks and reaching certain goals. Bandura (1986) outlined four determinants of self-efficacy: past success, vicarious learning (modeling), emotional or psychological state, and material and social resources.

When individuals experience past experiences with success, or mastery experiences, they are more likely to experience a sense of self-efficacy before attempting a specific task, if they have successfully completed similar activities in the past. Furthermore, successes foster self-efficacy only when individuals view these successes as a result of their personal effort or ability (Tolli and Schmidt 2008).

Vicarious learning or modeling can also affect self-efficacy. Individuals are more likely to have self-efficacy about performing a certain task after they have observed someone, whom they regard as similar to themselves, perform this task successfully. The emotional and physiological state of individuals can also influence the self-efficacy of individuals. For example, if individuals are anxious or nervous, they may feel vulnerable, and thus, their self-efficacy may be undermined. Material and social resources in the form of support from friends, colleagues, or relatives can influence self-efficacy.

Self-efficacy can be related to specific tasks, such as stopping abuse of a substance. Because self-efficacy reflects an individual's ability to achieve certain outcomes, it is believed to have a major role in behavior change (West and Hardy 2006).

Self-efficacy theory suggests that more people would attempt to enter treatment if they thought that the attempt would be successful (Wechsberg et al. 2007). Thus, Bandura's original theory has been applied to and adapted for addictive behaviors. Marlatt (1985) theorized that there are four psychosocial processes related to the addiction and relapse processes: self-efficacy, outcome expectancies, attributions of causality, and decision-making processes. Self-efficacy, relative to relapse, is the individual's ability to effectively cope with situations that carry a high risk of relapse. Outcome expectancies are an individual's expectations (both positive and negative) about the effects of an addictive substance. Attributions of causality refer to a person's beliefs about whether relapse is the result of internal or external causes. Substance use is the result of multiple decisions about using the substance and the risk for relapse.

Marlatt and Gordon's (1985) model proposed that self-efficacy in terms of addictive behavior was influenced by the interrelationship between environmental factors (e.g., drug availability, peers, etc.) and psychological factors (e.g., cognition, affect, coping, etc.) that determine whether relapse will occur. Thus, this model emphasizes that cognitive interpretations and behavioral reactions to environmental events are relevant to the origins of substance abuse, maintaining addiction, and type of treatment intervention.

Self-efficacy to maintain abstinence and avoid relapse has been shown to play an important role in changing substance-related behavior, reducing substance use during treatment, and maintaining treatment progress (Benda 2002; Levin et al. 2007; Nes and Oei 2005). However, self-efficacy might be differentially related to treatment outcomes depending on the individual's level of self-cognition and self-evaluation.

Marlatt (1996) classified efficacy judgments in terms of stages of drug and alcohol misuse. *Resistance efficacy beliefs* are individuals' judgments of their ability to avoid substance abuse prior to first use. *Harm reduction self-efficacy beliefs* are individuals' judgments about their ability to reduce substance use once they become addicted. Marlatt (1996) postulated that craving and self-efficacy are related, and high levels of craving are more detrimental to the individual's coping skills. Marlatt (1985) defined *craving* as "a motivational state associated with a strong desire for an expected positive outcome" (p.

138). Thus, it is believed that giving up the substance has a positive effect on an individual's self-efficacy (West and Hardy 2006).

An updated relapse prevention model (Witkiewitz and Marlatt 2004) proposed that low self-efficacy makes individuals vulnerable to relapse, which may be aggravated by poor coping skills.

Summary

CBT incorporates both behavioral theory and cognitive theory (Carroll and Onkin 2005). Like cognitive therapy, CBT emphasizes analyzing the current problematic situation of substance abusers and their thoughts and reactions associated with substance abuse (Beck et al. 2005). However, it goes beyond analysis and changing the substance abusers' thinking about themselves in relationship to substance abuse and also endeavors to change abusers' coping behaviors (Beck et al. 2005).

Attribution, appraisals, self-efficacy, and expectancies are elements of cognitive theory included in cognitive-behavioral therapy. The key objective of CBT is to modify thoughts associated with substance abuse and to develop new behaviors to replace dysfunctional behaviors (Beck et al. 2005) and to prevent relapse (Ball 2007; Marlatt 1985, 1996; Miller and Carpenter 2005).

Self-efficacy theory originated from social cognitive theory and posits that individuals with self-efficacy perceive themselves as capable of performing certain tasks and reaching certain goals (Bandura 1986, 1987). Bandura (1986) outlined four determinants of self-efficacy: past success, vicarious learning (modeling), emotional or psychological state, and material and social resources. As applied to substance abuse, *self-efficacy* refers to individuals' confidence in their ability to resist using substances.

Bandura's (1986) original theory has been applied to and adapted for addictive behaviors by Marlatt (1985, 1996).

According to Marlatt (1985), there are four psychosocial processes related to the addiction and relapse processes: self-efficacy, outcome expectancies, attributions of causality, and decision-making processes. Marlatt and Gordon's (1985) model emphasizes that cognitive interpretations and behavioral reactions to environmental events are relevant to the origins of substance abuse, maintaining addiction, and type of treatment intervention. Marlatt (1996) classified efficacy judgments in terms of stages of drug and alcohol misuse and used the terms *resistance efficacy beliefs* (individuals' judgments of their ability to avoid substance abuse prior to first use) and *harm reduction self-efficacy beliefs* (individuals' judgments about their ability to reduce substance use once they become addicted).

An updated relapse prevention model (Witkiewitz and Marlatt 2004) proposed that low self-efficacy makes individuals vulnerable to relapse, which may be aggravated by poor coping skills.

In chapter 3, CBT and empirical research related to CBT and substance abuse treatment will be examined in more detail. The components of self-evaluation and self-cognition will also be discussed.

CHAPTER THREE

Cognitive Behavioral Therapy: Theory and Related Research

Introduction and Overview

Behavioral interventions for drug and alcohol dependence have been tested in several controlled clinical trials (e.g., Robinson et al., 2006). Self-evaluation and self-cognition have been shown to contribute to an accurate functional analysis of behavior and eventual recovery (Litt et al., 2008). Self-evaluation and self-cognition can also help individuals develop the self-efficacy to overcome substance abuse. CBT helps abusers recognize and cope with their addictive behavior. In this chapter self-evaluation, self-cognition, and CBT and substance abuse treatment will be discussed.

Self-Evaluation

Numerous studies that have investigated drug use have relied on self-evaluations (Diaz et al. 2008; Richter and Johnson, 2001; Rosay, Najaka, and Herz 2007; Stasiewicz et al. 2008). Richter and Johnson(2001) discussed the various methods of assessing and measuring substance use behaviors and the advantages and disadvantages of self-evaluation instruments. Richter and Johnson (2001) described the various methods of administering self-evaluation measures, including self-administration with paper and pencil questionnaires, computer assisted self-interviews or interactive voice recording, and through personal interviews conducted by an interviewer.

The advantages of self-evaluation measures are ease of administration to large samples, ease of simultaneous administration in different locations, quantifiability and analyzability of responses, and offer the ability opportunity for the researcher to question respondents about different areas of interest. Respondents may also choose to skip items that they do not wish to answer; this ensures integrity and ethics of the data by allowing respondents to decide what they wish or do not wish to reveal (Richter and Johnson 2001).

The disadvantages to self-evaluation measures have to do with their validity and reliability. Drug use is a sensitive topic, and self-evaluation of drug use lends itself to questionable validity of self-reported data is questionable, especially when the topic is as sensitive as drug use. For instance, individuals in the criminal justice system may be reluctant to self-evaluate because they fear negative consequences (Rosay et al. 2007). Self-evaluation measures allow respondents to answer according to how they believe the researcher wants them to respond and not according to their true feelings. Because respondents may want to present themselves and their behaviors as socially desirable, they may alter their true responses (Richter and Johnson 2001; Rosay et al. 2007). In some cases, respondents may want to present negative pictures of themselves, possibly for amusement or to gain attention for a particular intervention (Richter and Johnson 2001).

Another disadvantage is that unintentional errors where respondents are unable to recall information accurately, interviewing methodology errors, drug misidentification, and psychopharmacological effects of drug use may affect the validity of self-evaluations (Diaz et al. 2008; Rosay et al. 2007).

Stasiewicz et al.'s (2008) study examined subject-collateral self-evaluation reports of alcohol abuse among a sample of 167 individuals dually diagnosed with bipolar disorder and alcohol abuse or dependence at an outpatient treatment facility at a community mental health clinic. Subjects were recruited within two weeks of entering treatment and completed measures of cognitive functioning, alcohol dependence severity, psychiatric symptoms, and quantity and frequency of substance use over the previous sixty days using the Timeline Follow-Back interview (Sobell and Sobell 1996, as cited in Stasiewicz et al. 2008).

Subjects also provided a urine sample for screening for recent drug use. Collateral interviews were conducted by phone and included an assessment of the subject's alcohol and drug use over the same sixty-day period. Collaterals expressed confidence in the accuracy of their reports. The findings indicated inconsistency between subjects and collaterals. However, there was greater subject-collateral consistency for individuals (N = 97) with negative urine drug screens. Thus, subjects' recent drug use was the most consistent predictor of subject-collateral discrepancy scores.

Despite the imperfect nature of self-evaluation, this technique and associated measures are often preferred over biological testing, such as urinalysis, because they are more practical, less intrusive, and less expensive (Rosay et al. 2007). In addition, self-evaluations tell more about the extent of drug use, such as duration, frequency, intensity, and other patterns of drug use (Diaz, Horton et al. 2008; Rosay et al. 2007).

Self-Cognition

McCusker (2001) observed that approaches to the treatment of substance abuse are based on cognitive bias; that is, abusers' behaviors are the result of a biased belief system about their ability to refrain from substance abuse and that interventions aim to restructure the abuser's beliefs. These altered beliefs form the basis of motivation to refrain from substance abuse and from relapse. These cognitive biases are an important consideration in self-cognition for a number of reasons.

First, as McCusker (2001) noted, abuser's beliefs or expectancies assumed to be true may influence ongoing behavior automatically without conscious awareness. Therefore, self-cognition may not give the entire picture about the cognitive processes and beliefs involved in an addictive behavior. If such behaviors are automatic, and therefore assumed to be unconscious, they do not easily lend themselves to accurate self-cognition. As a result, while the individual's self-cognition may have some value, it will be limited.

Second, McCusker pointed out that access to information stored in an individual's memory is activated by cues and situations. With respect to substance abuse and addiction, individuals may be aware of triggers, but their ability to self-evaluate may be hampered by cognitive bias. Therefore, accessible or reported self-cognition information activated by cues in research situations may not be the same as that in substance abuse contexts.

McCusker (2001) argued for investigating cognitive biases in the addictions that are based on cognitive science and cognitive neuropsychology methods, which go beyond what individuals say and make inferences about cognitive processes and structures based on behavioral responses. Such methods directly assess the propositions and processes of memory that are assumed to motivate ongoing behavior rather than the individual's self-perception of behavior, exert less demands because no direct inquiry about reasons for behavior is made, and are not made, and access aspects of cognition that are generally not part of self-cognition.

Where McCusker (2001) is more theoretical in his views and comes more from the perspective of therapists, Robinson et al. (2006) approached self-cognition empirically from the perspective of users. Robinson et al. noted that unlike physical healthcare, where patients' self-cognitions often form the basis of treatment and treatment outcomes, within mental healthcare, clients' views of their problems in their own words rarely form the basis for measuring the outcome of therapy.

According to Robinson et al. (2006), current self-cognition measures (e.g., Clinical Outcomes Routine Evaluation—Outcome Measure [CORE-OM]) are based on measures, such as the Beck Depression Inventory (BDI), that identify and assess the origins of mental illness. Further, individuals' responses on these instruments are categorized according to a specific psychiatric or psychotherapeutic linguistic framework and not in the individuals' own words.

Robinson et al. (2006) described an outcome measure, Psychological Outcome Profiles (PSYCHLOPS), which they used with 235 users of primary care mental health services recruited through four therapists working in southeast England. PSYCHLOPS asks individuals to describe, in their own words, "the problem that troubles you most," "another problem," and to "choose one thing that is hard to do because of your problem" (p. 167). Individuals' responses allowed Robinson et al. to explore how clients conceptualize their most troubling problem and its consequences and to provide a typology of these responses.

Seven thematic categories emerged for the *problem domain*: interpersonal, past event, state of mind, somatic, self-evaluation, competence/performance, and material issues. Six themes emerged from the *consequences of the problem domain* responses: competence/ performance, interpersonal, frame of mind, resolution and progression, self-evaluation, and somatic.

While Robinson et al.'s (2006) study did not investigate substance abuse and substance abuse treatment in particular, the results can be applied to substance abuse treatment in terms of the use of narrative in self-cognition. Individuals in treatment for substance abuse have a variety of stories that represent their own unique experiences. Their narratives can help frame substance abuse-related problems in personal and social contexts that can be useful in clinical and therapeutic contexts.

Cognitive Behavioral Therapy and Substance Abuse Treatment

Numerous studies (Carroll 1996, 1998; Carroll, Rounsaville, Gordon, et al. 1994; Carroll, Rounsaville, Nich, et al. 1994; Marlatt 1985) have provided empirical support for the use of CBT to treat substance abuse. For example, a study conducted by Aharonovich et al. (2008) provided empirical support for use of CBT in treating cocaine dependence. Aharonovich et al. examined patients' cognitive abilities and verbal expressions of commitment to behavioral change as predictors of retention of treatment-related information and drug use outcomes in an outpatient CBT of adult cocaine-dependent patients.

A computerized neuropsychological battery was administered at the time of entering treatment entry to test patients' neurocognitive functioning and to establish a baseline. Two independent raters used recordings of CBT sessions to code commitment language strength across the temporal segments (e.g., beginning, middle, and end) of one session per patient. The findings revealed that better cognitive abilities were a predictor of treatment retention, but not drug use. Mean commitment strength across the session segments was a predictor of reduced drug use. Commitment to behavioral changes, such as abstinence, may occur independently of patients' cognitive abilities; in other words, a strong commitment to abstinence can overcome any cognitive impairments. However, the client's engagement in the behavioral intervention process and cognitive abilities are related. Clients with cognitive impairments may not be as engaged in the intervention.

Rawson et al. (2006) compared the efficacy of contingency management (CM) and CBT for the treatment of stimulant abusers, both alone and in combination. Participants were 177 individuals who abused cocaine. Participants were randomly assigned to one of the three study conditions: CM ($N = 60$), CBT ($N = 58$) or combined CM and CBT ($N = 59$). All interventions lasted sixteen weeks. CM participants were required to provide three urine samples per week and meet briefly (two to five minutes) with the CM technician.

The CBT procedure consisted of forty-eight ninety-minute group sessions (three per week for sixteen weeks). Individuals in this treatment condition participated in both the CM procedure and the CBT groups, which were delivered simultaneously and not integrated. Participants were interviewed at baseline and weeks seventeen, twenty-six, and fifty-two. Measures included psychiatric disorders and alcohol and drug use and concomitant social problems.

The findings indicated that CM procedures produced better retention and lower rates of stimulant use during the study period. Self-reported stimulant use was reduced from baseline levels at all follow-up points for all groups, and urinalysis data did not differ between groups at follow-up. While CM produced robust evidence of efficacy during treatment application, CBT produced comparable longer-term outcomes. Combination of CM and CBT produced no evidence of an additive effect.

Summary

While practitioners recognize that substance abuse is a function of numerous physiological and genetic elements, they believe that addiction is a learned behavior and that behavior can be changed using treatment techniques based on self-evaluation and self-cognition (McCusker 2001; Robinson et al. 2006). Self-evaluation and self-cognition have been shown to contribute to an accurate functional analysis of behavior and eventual recovery (Litt et al. 2008). Cognitive therapies, such as CBT, have as a goal changing the belief systems that underlie substance abuse (McCusker 2001), and this goal has been supported by numerous empirical studies (Carroll 1996, 1998; Carroll, Rounsaville, Gordon, et al. 1994; Carroll, Rounsaville, Nich, et al. 1994; Marlatt 1985).

Aharonovich et al.'s (2008) study evidenced a connection between cognitive ability, commitment to abstinence, and engagement in intervention, and found that cognitive ability did not affect commitment but did affect the level of the individual's engagement in the substance abuse intervention.

Rawson et al.'s (2006) study that compared the efficacy of CM and CBT for the treatment of stimulant abusers found that CBT was more efficacious over the longer term. Despite this evidence, those struggling with substance abuse may have difficulty with abstinence and may relapse.

In chapter 4, self-efficacy theory and empirical research related to self-efficacy and substance abuse treatment will be examined in more detail. Constructs of the self and definitions of self-efficacy will also be discussed.

Chapter Four

Self-Efficacy Theory and Research Applications to Substance Abuse Treatment

Introduction and Overview

In the previous chapter, the influence of the individual's level of self-cognition and self-evaluation to CBT treatment outcomes was discussed. An individual's self-construct or self-schema holds specific beliefs about self-efficacy and results in behaviors according to these beliefs. Self-efficacy can be defined in terms of several factors, including socialization (Galliher, Evans, and Weiser 2007), ethnic identity and spirituality (Wong and Longshore 2008), and life stress factors (Tate et al. 2008).

In this chapter, self-efficacy theory and empirical research related to self-efficacy and substance abuse treatment will be examined in more detail. Constructs of the self and definitions of self-efficacy as addressed in empirical research studies will also be discussed.

Constructs of the Self

In the previous chapter, McCusker's (2001) observation that substance abusers have cognitive biases that affect their treatment was discussed. In addition, it was noted, respondents to self-evaluation measures may not always respond truthfully, either because they wish to present themselves and their behaviors as socially desirable (Richter and Johnson 2001; Rosay et al. 2007) or present themselves negatively for a variety of reasons (Richter and Johnson 2001).

Rudman and Spencer (2007) may offer an answer to self-cognition and self-evaluation issues in their advocacy of understanding the implicit views of the self. Doing so requires going beyond explicit measures, such as questionnaires and other measurement instruments, which may lead to cognitive bias and may be limited by respondents' accurate assessment to true knowledge of the self.

According to Rudman and Spencer (2007), "If people cannot accurately introspect about themselves, then even under the best of circumstances, self-reports can only tell us what people believe to be true" (p. 97).

Koole and Coenen's findings about the implicit self (2007) are particularly relevant to substance abusers and substance abuse treatment. Koole and Coenen (2007) found that the implicit self plays a significant role in automatic emotion regulation. For individuals who are action-oriented, subliminally priming the implicit self helps to down-regulate negative emotions. For state-oriented individuals, activating the implicit self incurs the persistence of negative emotions. For practitioners, these findings provide a better understanding of what types of individuals are able to resist negative thinking and feelings.

Margolin, Schuman-Olivier, Beitel, Arnold, Fulwiler, and Avants (2007) viewed the self from a spiritual perspective in their study of HIV-positive drug users. A self-schema is conceptualized as a highly automatized system of knowledge or beliefs about one's intentions and abilities stored in long-term memory. Activation of the self-schema leads to activation of specific beliefs and behaviors in accordance with these beliefs. The goal of 3-S therapy is "to facilitate a shift in the habitually activated self-schema of the addicted individual, which, when triggered, leads to impulsive harmful behavior" (Margolin et al. 2007, p. 982).

Therapy incorporating self-schema theory is relevant to the treatment of substance abuse, as addiction has been characterized as overlearned negative behaviors that overcome all other behaviors and create an addict self-schema or self-construct.

According to Margolin et al. (2007), increased HIV risk behavior in drug-abusing patient populations is a function of impulsivity that can be modified by mindfulness-based psychotherapies incorporating spiritual self-schema (3-S) therapy that will move HIV-positive drug users away from the habitual activation of the maladaptive and potentially destructive addict self-schema to a spiritual self-schema, defined by individuals according to their own religious or spiritual tradition and beliefs, that fosters mindfulness, compassion, and doing no harm to self and others.

Definition of Self-Efficacy

Previous chapters have presented the definition of self-efficacy from a theoretical perspective. Efficacy is generally conceptualized as perceived competence for executing specific behaviors in a specific situation. In the context of substance abuse, self-efficacy can be defined in terms of socialization factors (Galliher et al. 2007), ethnic identity and spirituality (Wong and Longshore 2008), and life stress factors (Tate et al. 2008).

In their study of Native American youth and substance abuse, Galliher et al. (2007) examined the possibility of indirect effects of the primary socialization sources of family, school, and peers on substance use in eighty-four Native American children between the ages of nine and eleven living on a reservation. Galliher et al. hypothesized that these socialization sources predicted self-efficacy, drug use, and drug refusal. Galliher et al. found that school bonding and peer social skills predicted self-efficacy, while family predicted refusal skills. Parental acceptance or support was not related to self-efficacy nor were peer social skills related to refusal skills. Both self-efficacy and refusal skills predicted drug use or experimentation.

Wong and Longshore (2008) examined the factors of ethnic identity and spirituality on substance abuse treatment outcomes in 114 Hispanic Americans enrolled in methadone maintenance treatment and the extent to which self-efficacy influenced treatment outcomes. Higher levels of self-efficacy at intake predicted higher probability of heroin abstinence and a lower number of drugs used at one-year follow-up. Greater levels of ethnic identity were related to greater levels of self-efficacy and lowers levels of substance use.

Tate et al. (2008) examined life stress and self-efficacy as predictors of time to relapse for 113 adults with comorbid major depressive disorder and alcohol or substance dependence. Life stress, self-efficacy, and substance use were assessed at treatment entry, twelve weeks (mid-treatment), and twenty-four weeks (end of treatment).

Participants were enrolled in a randomized clinical trial comparing integrated cognitive behavioral therapy (ICBT) and twelve-step facilitation therapy (TSF) for comorbid substance dependence and depression. Time to relapse was defined as the number of days from treatment initiation until first alcohol or drug use.

Within the twenty-four-week study period, Tate et al. (2008) found that half of the sample relapsed. There was no significant difference between ICBT and TSF groups. Individuals experiencing life stressors were more likely to relapse earlier than those not experiencing life stressors. The interaction of self-efficacy and life stress was not significant; however, individuals with higher levels of self-efficacy maintained abstinence from alcohol and drugs longer than those with lower levels of self-efficacy.

Self-Efficacy and Substance Abuse Treatment

Efficacy has therapeutic value because its effects can be generalized to the treatment of substance abuse. Several researchers (i.e., Levin et al. 2007; Litt, Kadden, and Stephens 2005; Shadel and Cervone 2006) have demonstrated the generalizability of efficacy using various methodological approaches. Levin et al. (2007) examined the relationship between abstinence self-efficacy and cognitive components of coping (positive reappraisal and cognitive avoidance) for 2,596 participants from fifteen residential substance use disorder treatment programs in the Veterans Affairs health care system. Participants were assessed at treatment entry, discharge, and five-year follow-up.

At five years, abstinence self-efficacy predicted posttreatment alcohol use. There was a significant relationship between self-efficacy and levels of alcohol use and levels of alcohol dependence symptoms. There were no significant main effects for positive reappraisal coping or interaction effects between self-efficacy and positive reappraisal coping.

Cognitive avoidance coping moderated the effects of self-efficacy on alcohol use at five years, whereas positive reappraisal coping was largely unrelated to outcomes. Individuals with low self-efficacy who relied on avoidance coping strategies had poorer alcohol use outcomes; however, as self-efficacy increased, the negative influence of avoidance coping strategies decreased.

Litt et al. (2005) examined whether substance use outcomes in a large-scale study of marijuana treatment could be accounted for by changes in coping skills or by other variables central to CBT, such as readiness or self-efficacy. Participants were 450 men and women treated in the multisite Marijuana Treatment Project and were randomly assigned to motivational enhancement therapy plus cognitive–behavioral (MET-CB) treatment, motivational enhancement therapy (MET), or a delayed treatment control group. Marijuana use and coping skills were measured at baseline and at follow-ups through fifteen months.

Litt et al. (2005) found that marijuana outcomes were predicted by treatment type and by coping skills used. The coping-skills-oriented MET-CB treatment did not result in greater use of coping skills than the MET treatment. Change in self-efficacy was strongly related to change in the percentage of days the participant smoked marijuana (PDS) in the ninety days prior to each assessment point, periods (quarters) per day in which smoking occurred (PPD), joints per day smoked (JPD), and continuous abstinence for the ninety-day period prior to follow-up. Baseline readiness to change was not related to any of these outcome measures.

Litt et al. (2005) concluded that self-efficacy changes drove the coping changes that helped decrease substance use.

Shadel and Cervone's (2006) study examined both self-efficacy and self-schema in treatment of smokers. Thirty-eight regular smokers participated individually in four weekly smoking cessation sessions, each held at the same time of day. Session 1 assessed the content of the smoker self-schema—abstainer ideal-possible self and abstainer ought-possible self—to develop the cognitive priming manipulations. A different one of each of the three self-schemas was then primed during Sessions 2, 3, and 4, and participants were exposed to both craving conditions after exposure to each priming condition (all conditions were presented in counterbalanced order among participants to avoid order effects).

The data revealed that self-efficacy to resist smoking in high-risk situations (i.e., situations that provoke high levels of craving) is regulated by cognitive knowledge structures or self-schemas that influence abstinence. Cognitively priming both of these abstainer selves increased self-efficacy and decreased craving compared with when a smoking-related self-schema was cognitively primed under the same provocative cue conditions. There was a relationship between self-efficacy and cravings. Higher levels of self-efficacy were consistently related to decreased craving.

Summary

Self-constructs, or self-schema, play a significant role in substance abuse and treatment of substance abuse.

Koole and Coenen (2007) found that the implicit self plays a significant role in automatic emotion regulation. For practitioners working with substance abusers, knowledge of the implicit self provides a better understanding of what types of individuals are able to resist negative thinking and feelings.

An individual's self-construct or self-schema is related to self-efficacy and results in behaviors according to these beliefs. Self-efficacy can be defined in terms of several factors, including socialization (Galliher et al. 2007), ethnic identity and spirituality (Wong and Longshore 2008), and life stress factors (Tate et al. 2008), which can influence treatment outcomes and coping skills (Levin et al. 2007; Litt et al. 2005; Shadel and Cervone 2006).

In chapter 5, models of substance abuse treatment will be discussed. Specifically, the literature relevant to the disease and relapse prevention treatment models will be examined.

CHAPTER FIVE

Models of Substance Abuse Treatment

Introduction and Overview

In the previous chapter, self-efficacy theory and empirical research related to self-efficacy and substance abuse treatment were examined. Constructs of the self and definitions of self-efficacy as addressed in empirical research studies were discussed.

Historically, the disease model of addiction posited that substance use is a biological lifelong disease aggravated by environmental condition. In this model, individuals are viewed as helpless in controlling their substance abuse behaviors and must depend on others to do so (Ouimette et al. 1997).

In the relapse prevention model, (Marlatt and Gordon 1985), individuals are active participants in overcoming substance abuse by making appropriate decisions and utilizing appropriate coping skills. There is also a growing body of literature about the role of emotion regulation in the treatment of substance abuse.

In this chapter, research relative to the disease model of substance abuse and the relapse prevention model will be discussed. Research on emotional regulation and substance abuse is also presented.

Disease Models

Since the 1970s, substance abuse has generally been defined as a disease, as opposed to a moral or character weakness, and that substance misuse is caused by a fundamental biological or psychological susceptibility that results in an individual's loss of control of consumption of the misused substance (Fisher and Roget 2008). This model is the basis of the twelve-step treatment programs, in which participants are instructed to accept the disease model of substance abuse, identify themselves as addicts, and seek abstinence as a goal (Ouimette et al. 1997).

Traditional substance abuse treatment programs based on the disease model tend to be confrontative and attempt to break through individuals' defenses and give them a realistic look at their addiction disease. Individuals are then built back up as sober persons with sober lifestyles (De Leon 1995; Hartel and Glantz 1999).

The confrontation group is one technique used. Individuals are seated in the center of a circle of group members, who confront them about perceived character flaws that prevent them from viewing their problems realistically. Individuals must declare that they are addicts before any work begins. Relapse is often a sign that individuals are not ready for treatment. If individuals do relapse, they may be discharged from treatment to help them decide whether to eventually reseek treatment when they are truly ready (Marlatt, Blume, and Parks 2001).

The development of substance abuse treatment based on the disease model is unique because it evolved in relative isolation from mainstream health care (Guydish 2003; White 1998). Through the middle of the twentieth century, little or no professional help was available for substance abuse treatment, which often carried a social stigma.

As a result, an alternative system of care, provided primarily by compassionate peers who were themselves in recovery, arose. Although based on a disease model, substance abuse treatment remained separate in specialized treatment programs that had little or no connection to medical and mental health services. Treatment practices, such as those used in Alcoholics Anonymous and twelve-step programs, were based on the intuition and wisdom of those recovering from substance abuse (Ouimette et al. 1997). Individual substance abuse treatment providers, programs, and systems adhered strongly to particular treatment models even if they empirical evidence of efficacy (Morgenstern 2000). This fueled a broader debate about the merits of relying on evidence-based practices in behavioral health services (Beutler 2004; Levant 2004).

In light of this debate, attempts are being made to provide empirical evidence for substance abuse treatment. One notable study is Matto's (2007) study of a twelve-week treatment protocol for chronic substance abuse patients. This was the first empirical study about the implementation of a protocol that combined CBT techniques with sensory-based visual exposure and processing strategies and the effect on the ability to regulate emotions with adult patients in a public inpatient mental health facility.

According to Matto, there is a need to further develop innovative multimodal integrated treatment protocols for the heterogeneous addiction population. Integrated treatments that include a sensory component may be particularly effective for substance abuse clients struggling with chronic dependence or other extreme stress conditions (p. 44).

The sample size in this study was eight individuals ranging in age from twenty-two to fifty-six years. A treatment team identified substance dependence as a primary clinical issue. Treatment duration ranged from two weeks to thirteen months, with an average length of stay of five months. All individuals were receiving medication for another mental health disorder, which included panic disorder, schizophrenia, schizoaffective disorder, bipolar, and major depression. The study employed a pre-post design, with all clients attending at least eight to ten of the twelve group sessions.

Posttreatment measures showed significant change on several emotional regulation capacity dimensions. Specifically, results showed an increase in emotional expression and verbalization of emotions related to participants' substance abuse and an increase in social interaction, as reported by clinicians. The data showed a significant decrease in clients' urge or desire to drink alcohol or use drugs, as reported by participants. Changes in reduction in stress and anxiety related to participants' substance abuse, general emotional or physical discomfort related to addiction triggers, or improvement in thinking skills used to feel better when addiction triggers were activated were not statistically significant.

Matto (2007) concluded that affect regulation is an important component to managing cue reactivity and preventing relapse, as research shows that significant changes in the brain resulting from direct exposure to drugs and from stress may lead to relapse by inhibiting the cognitive control resources needed for effective behavioral decision making. The visual-verbal processing protocol based on CBT offered an integrated and innovative approach to helping individuals who abuse substances manage and verbalize emotions and decrease cravings.

Matto's (2007) study offers the empirical evidence for substance abuse treatment that is currently lacking. It is based not on a disease model, but on a relapse prevention treatment model, which is discussed in the next section.

Relapse Prevention Treatment Model

Marlatt and Gordon's (1985) CBT model of relapse prevention is a wide-used substance abuse treatment (Ball 2007). The model extended Bandura's (1986, 1997) theory of self-efficacy. Four psychological processes related to addiction and relapse underlie this model: self-efficacy, outcome expectancies, attributions of causality, and decision-making processes.

With respect to relapse situations, *self-efficacy* refers to one's ability to deal competently and effectively with situations where this is a high risk of relapse. *Outcome expectancies* refer to a person's expectations about the effects of an addictive substance (e.g., changes in mood, perceptions, or behavior). *Attributions of causality* refer to a person's beliefs about whether relapse is the result of internal or external causes.

Substance use is the result of multiple decisions about using the substance and that may place the user at risk for relapse.

Futterman et al. (2005) described a relapse prevention treatment program, the Growth and Recovery Program, based on Marlatt and Gordon's (1985) model. This model emphasizes working on the process of behaviors in session and integrates recent developments in psychological theory and technique (i.e., CBT and psychodynamic) into a harm reduction framework.

In the Growth and Recovery Program, each individual with substance abuse problem work with a social worker, also known as the person's care coordinator, a psychiatrist, a psychologist, and a vocational rehabilitation counselor. The components of the Growth and Recovery Program include vocational groups, recovery groups (either didactic groups about the twelve-step model of treatment and relapse prevention techniques or psychodynamic therapy groups about recovery issues), group psychotherapy (including a men's and a women's group), community meetings, cognitive–behavioral skills training groups (e.g., anger management and stress reduction), and ear acupuncture. The social worker (care coordinator) engages the individual and helps him or her with social service issues, medical follow-up, substance abuse, and other counseling. A psychiatrist prescribes medication, and a psychologist provides individual psychotherapy in addition to the social worker's counseling. A vocational rehabilitation counselor sees patients individually and in groups.

Individuals attend the program from 9:00 a.m. to 1:00 p.m., three to five days a week, depending on the intensity of the treatment needed and the scheduling demands of individuals. Patients attend three groups a day. This schedule is customized to the individual needs of the patient, allowing for flexibility to coordinate outside medical or social service appointments. Supervised urine samples are taken daily, and breathalyzers are used as indicated. Individuals remain in the from six months to one year before entering an aftercare program, which can consist of weekly or biweekly sessions with their care coordinator and may be combined with an aftercare group, individual therapy, or visits with the vocational counselor as needed (Futterman et al. 2005).

According to Futterman et al. (2005), relapse prevention is a more low-key approach that assumes relapse is a natural and predictable part of the recovery process. Therefore, program participants are encouraged to discuss each relapse, analyze how it happened, and work toward preventing the next relapse. Individuals determine the thoughts and behaviors, or triggers, that preceded the relapse and plan ways to recognize them and intervene early.

Summary

Substance abuse has generally been defined as a disease with a biological or psychological origin. Treatment programs are usually confrontative and require the participants to admit that they have an addiction disease and to endeavor to abstain from the substance (De Leon 1995; Hartel and Glantz 1999).

Relapse is viewed as a sign that individuals are not ready for treatment and they may be discharged from treatment until they are ready to overcome their disease (Marlatt et al. 2001).

The disease model of substance abuse evolved in isolation from the mainstream medical field (Guydish 2003; White 1998) and has sparked debate about the lack of empirical evidence of the efficacy of treatment based on this model.

Matto's (2007) study is significant because it was one of the first to offer empirical evidence about a substance abuse treatment model. The study is also significant because it addressed emotional regulation and relapse prevention. Futterman et al.'s (2005) study also addressed relapse prevention, integrating CBT and psychodynamics into a harm reduction framework and working behavioral processes in session.

In chapter 6, a substance abuse treatment program based on CBT, self-efficacy, self-evaluation, and self-cognition will be presented. Specifically, in chapter 6, the research question of the study, based on current research and theory—What components of CBT and self-efficacy theory might logically be included in a treatment program that focuses on reducing substance abuse using self-cognition and self-evaluation methods?—will be answered.

CHAPTER SIX

A Substance Abuse Treatment Program Based on Cognitive Behavioral Therapy, Self-Efficacy, Self-Evaluation, and Self-Cognition

Introduction and Overview

In chapter 5, research relative to the disease model of substance abuse and the relapse prevention model were discussed, and research on emotional regulation and substance abuse was also presented.

CBT combines both cognitive and behavioral theories and forms the foundation for comprehensive approach to substance abuse treatment. A broader range of cognitions, which were identified by Marlatt and Gordon (1985) as attributions, appraisals, self-efficacy expectancies, and substance-related effect expectancies, are included in CBT.

In this chapter, a substance abuse treatment program based on CBT is presented.

Program Goals and Strategies

Individuals' appraisals of stressful situations, self-efficacy in coping with such situations, and avoiding relapse after discontinuing substance abuse are important in substance abuse treatment (Marlatt and Gordon 1985; Wong and Longshore 2008). The research question posed for this study was What components of CBT and self-efficacy theory might logically be included in a treatment program that focuses on reducing substance abuse using self-cognition and self-evaluation methods?

In response to this question, an intervention is developed that has as an overarching goal of reducing substance abuse by helping participants become more aware of their feelings and reactions and changing them in ways that will support cessation of substance abuse.

The strategies of this intervention program, adapted from Matto (2007) and McCusker (2001), are to

1. help clients capture thoughts, feelings, sensations;
2. identify and label feelings;
3. identify positive and negative expectancies of substance abuse;
4. demonstrate awareness of triggers for substance abuse;
5. seek out alternative interpretations of substance abuse thoughts and behaviors; and
6. modify existing cognitive structures.

Model Program

Early behavioral strategies for treatment of substance focused primarily on overt, observable behaviors and understanding the triggers and reinforcement elements of substance abuse to explain and modify behavior. In other words, these strategies were nonmediational (Marlatt and Donovan 2005). However, strategies have evolved to include cognitive factors into conceptualizations of substance abuse and have become meditational; that is, substance abuse is attributed to the interaction among a number of a variables, such as individuals' beliefs, values, perceptions, expectations, and attributional processes, influencing whether individuals develop substance abuse problems and either continue or cease abusing substances (Marlatt and Donovan 2005; McCusker 2001).

This model intervention will incorporate the broader range of cognitions that are included in CBT, the concept of self-efficacy, and the strategies of self-evaluation and self-cognition.

Assessment, Screening, and Intake

Lazarus and Folkman (1994) described two different levels of cognitive appraisal: primary and secondary. Primary appraisal is the individual's perception of a situation and an estimate of stress, personal challenge, or threat related to the situation. Secondary appraisal is individual's evaluation of his or her ability to meet the challenges and demands to the situation. Secondary appraisal is important in every stressful encounter because it is influenced by the extent, nature, and availability of the individual's coping skills. This influence, in turn, mediates the individual's perception of stress and the emotional response (Folkman and Moskowitz 2000; Lazarus and Folkman 1994).

Participants in this intervention will meet the Diagnostic and Statistical Manual version IV (DSM-IV) (APA 2000) criteria for substance abuse. The age range of the participants will be twenty-five to fifty, the approximate age range of participants in Matto's (2007) study.

Participants will be asked at intake to indicate on a scale of 0-10 (0 = none and 10 = all the time) their self-ratings of

1. desire or urge for a substance,
2. stress or anxiety experienced when thinking about using a substance,
3. emotional discomfort experienced when thinking about using a substance,
4. physical discomfort experienced when thinking about using a substance, and
5. ability to feel better by thinking different thoughts when bothered by addiction triggers.

Duration of Therapy and Frequency of Sessions

Participants will attend twelve sessions of therapy, as CBT typically lasts for twelve sessions (Carroll 1998). Sessions will occur twice a week for approximately thirty minutes. Therefore, the therapy will last for six weeks. Therapy sessions will follow a format consistent with CBT protocols and will include a review of the previous session's learning, formulating the agenda for the session, completing the agenda with in-session discussions and exercises, and reviewing of the session content (Otto et al. 2007). Below is the outline for each two-session week.

Week 1: Substance Abuse, Coping, and Self-Evaluation

Discuss participant's experience with substance abuse, coping strategies, and self-evaluation of reasons for substance abuse. The following guiding questions will be used:

1. What has your substance abuse cost you?
2. Think of everything you have done to control your substance abuse. Think of specific strategies and examples of instances where you have used these strategies.
3. Honestly evaluate how far each strategy has brought you closer to overcoming your substance abuse problem.

Exercise: What do you want your life to stand for?

Participants envision that they have died and are listening to what loved ones say about them in their absence. Participant is encouraged to think about what they would have wanted loves one to say (Twohig and Peterson 2008).

Week 2: Obstacles and Struggles

Ask participants to identify obstacles related to their ability to stop abusing substances.

Ask participants to describe how their experience as they struggle with substance abuse. Point out commonalities and patterns among all participants.

Use the following prompts as a guide:

1. Make a list of all of the roadblocks you encounter in trying to stop your substance abuse.
2. Make a list of all of the roadblocks you anticipate you will encounter.
3. How do you deal with cravings?

Have participants share ways in which they attempt to moderate, regulate, or solve their problems.

Competency exercise: Write down what you think is missing in your life and why (Twohig and Peterson, 2008).

Week 3: Control

Discuss control in relationship to substance abuse. Ask participants to describe situations where they used positive control, such as not relapsing, and negative controls, such as using substances to control undesirable feelings. Ask participants to describe their feelings about their use of positive and negative control.

Week 4: Self-understanding

Discuss how participants give themselves reasons for their substance abuse. Use the following prompts as a guide:

1. What reasons do you give yourself or others for your substance abuse?
2. What are some recent examples of your doing this?
3. How did you feel when you noticed yourself giving reasons?

Week 5: Acceptance

Discuss the following questions:

1. Are you OK or not?
2. What does OK mean to you?
3. Are you acceptable or not?
4. What does acceptable mean to you?
5. What do you choose to do with your life?

Empty chair exercise: In this exercise, a participant is asked to have a conversation with an empty chair that represents a person, a goal, a desired outcome, etc. The participant moves back and forth between both chairs, playing himself or herself and the other person. The object of the conversation is to reveal and explore the emotions that are attached to the person, a goal, a desired outcome, etc., and to find ways of taking personal responsibility for resolving conflict (Goldfried 2006; Hayes, Strosahl, and Wilson 2003).

In this session participants will explore issues involving substance abuse by playing both roles in a conversation, and observing and working with the feelings that arise during the conversation.

Week 6: Progress Report

Participants will be asked to again self-rate on a scale of 0 to 10 desire or urges for a substance, stress or anxiety experienced when thinking about using a substance, emotional and physical discomfort experienced when thinking about using a substance, and ability to feel better by thinking different thoughts when bothered by addiction triggers. The results from the posttest will be compared to the intake results and discussed in the sessions.

Summary

In the present study, the following reason question was posed: What components of CBT and self-efficacy theory might logically be included in a treatment program that focuses on reducing substance abuse using self-cognition and self-evaluation methods? This question is answered with the development of an intervention. The goal of which is to reduce substance abuse by helping participants become more aware of their feelings and reactions and changing them in ways that will support cessation of substance abuse. Strategies for the intervention program were adapted from Matto (2007) and

McCusker (2001) and include helping clients capture thoughts, feelings, and sensations, identify and label feelings, identify positive and negative expectancies of substance abuse, demonstrate awareness of triggers for substance abuse, seek out alternative interpretations of substance abuse thoughts and behaviors, and modify existing cognitive structures.

In the concluding chapter, the study findings and implications are presented. Recommendations for future research are also made.

Chapter Seven

Summary and Discussion

Introduction and Overview

In this concluding chapter, a general overview of the findings of the study in light of current knowledge and past research are presented. Recommendations for future research will also be made.

The Application of Cognitive Behavioral Therapy and Self-Efficacy to a Substance Abuse Treatment Program with a Focus on Self-Evaluation and Self-Cognition

The research question posed for this study was what components of CBT and self-efficacy theory might logically be included in a treatment program that focuses on reducing substance abuse using self-cognition and self-evaluation methods?

In response to this question, an intervention is developed that has as an overarching goal of reducing substance abuse by helping participants become more aware of their feelings and coping reactions and changing them in ways that will support cessation of substance abuse.

The strategies of this intervention program, adapted from Matto (2007) and McCusker (2001), are to

1. help clients capture thoughts, feelings, and sensations;
2. identify and label feelings;
3. identify positive and negative expectancies of substance abuse;
4. demonstrate awareness of triggers for substance abuse;
5. seek out alternative interpretations of substance abuse thoughts and behaviors; and
6. modify existing cognitive structures.

As noted in previous chapters, CBT integrates principles of behavioral and cognitive theories and is a more comprehensive approach to treating substance abuse (Carroll and Onkin 2005). Marlatt and Gordon (1985) identified a broader range of cognition in CBT relative to substance abuse (attributions, appraisals, self-efficacy expectancies, and substance-related effect expectancies).

In the intervention of this study, these ranges of cognition were addressed. The intervention is designed to challenge participants' attributional processes. In cases of relapse, participants are encouraged to deal with their emotions, identify relapse tendencies, and change them. Participants are helped to understand that they relapse—not because they are generally unable to make good choices, but that their relapse is due to a lack of appropriate coping skills in response to a particular situation. This helps change their cognitive structures and negative self-cognitions and self-evaluations to reduce their sense of helplessness and increase their sense of self-efficacy.

Participants are also urged to consider both the positive and negative effects of the substance. Substance abusers may tell themselves, "I'll feel more relaxed if I pop some valiums" without considering other effects, such as "They'll make me so drowsy that I won't be able to function." According to Marlatt (1985), this strategy can either change individuals' beliefs about the positive effects of the substance or call their attention to the negative effects.

Relapse prevention is also a component of this intervention. Marlatt and Gordon (1985) suggested encouraging substance abusers to lead a more balanced life by examining the ratio of an individual's "shoulds" in life (i.e., demands and obligations) to "wants" in life (i.e., pleasures and rewards). By doing so, individuals can identify any feelings of deprivation and resentment that may lead to relapse. An underlying element of this intervention is to help individuals find a better balance and increase involvement in pleasant and rewarding aspects of their lives and reduce stress that may come from demands and obligations.

Discussion

While CBT incorporates both behavioral theory and cognitive theory (Carroll and Onkin 2005), CBT goes beyond analyzing substance abusers' problems and focuses on the present and attempts to help substance abusers change their coping behaviors (Beck et al. 2005). CBT includes elements of attribution, appraisals, self-efficacy, and expectancies (Marlatt and Gordon 1985).

That practitioners recognize that the origins of substance abuse are physiological and genetic is evidence of how substance abuse has traditionally been defined as a disease with a biological or psychological origin. As such, treatment programs are usually confrontative and require the participants to admit that they have an addiction disease and to endeavor to abstain from the substance (De Leon 1995; Hartel and Glantz 1999).

Relapse means that individuals are not ready for treatment and they may be discharged from treatment until they are ready to overcome their disease (Marlatt et al. 2001).

Because the disease model of substance abuse evolved apart from mainstream medicine (Guydish 2003; White 1998), there has been much debate about the lack of empirical evidence of the efficacy of substance abuse treatment based on this model. Thus, practitioners also believe that addiction is a learned behavior that can be changed using treatment techniques based on self-evaluation and self-cognition (McCusker 2001; Robinson et al. 2006). According to Litt et al. (2008), self-evaluation and self-cognition contribute to an accurate functional analysis of behavior and eventual recovery.

To facilitate behavior change and recovery, the objective of CBT is to modify thoughts associated with substance abuse and to develop new behaviors to replace dysfunctional behaviors (Beck et al. 2005) and to prevent relapse (Ball 2007; Marlatt 1985, 1996; Miller and Carpenter 2005). This goal has been supported by numerous empirical studies (Aharonovich et al. 2008; Carroll 1996, 1998; Carroll, Rounsaville, Gordon, et al. 1994; Carroll, Rounsaville, Nich, et al. 1994; Marlatt 1985; Rawson et al. 2006).

Self-constructs, or self-schema, play a significant role in substance abuse and treatment of substance abuse because an individual's self-construct or self-schema is related to self-efficacy and results in behaviors according to these beliefs (Galliher et al. 2007; Tate et al. 2008; Wong and Longshore 2008). These beliefs influence treatment outcomes and coping skills (Levin et al. 2007; Litt et al. 2005; Shadel and Cervone 2006).

The thrust of the intervention in the study is an active one and requires active participation for most effective learning. Marlatt and Gordon's (1985) four ranges of cognition (attributions, appraisals, self-efficacy expectancies, and substance-related effect expectancies) are included. The intervention is designed to challenge participants' attributional processes, encourage them to cope with their emotions, identify relapse tendencies, and change them. Participants are also urged to consider both the positive and negative effects of the substance. The underlying rationale of this intervention is to help participants change their cognitive structures and negative self-cognitions and self-evaluations to reduce their sense of helplessness, increase their sense of self-efficacy, and balance the "shoulds" and "woulds" (Marlatt and Gordon 1985). Most importantly, this intervention emphasizes practicing behaviors in therapeutic sessions so that they can be applied to participants' lives outside of sessions.

Implications for Further Research

An important implication for further research is suggested in light of the debate about the lack of empirical research for substance abuse treatment models and by Matto's (2007) study. Further empirical research about the efficacy of substance abuse treatment based on disease models and on models of CBT is warranted and significant because it was one of the first to offer empirical evidence about a substance abuse treatment model. The study is also significant because it addressed emotional regulation and relapse prevention. Futterman et al.'s (2005) study also addressed relapse prevention, integrating CBT and psychodynamics into a harm reduction framework and working behavioral processes in session.

This intervention described in this study emphasized practicing behaviors in therapeutic sessions so that they can be applied to participants' lives outside of sessions. This suggests another avenue for further research; namely, research on strategies that therapists and counselors can employ to help substance abusers reconcile adaptive attitudes and behaviors shown in sessions with maladaptive attitudes and behaviors that substance abusers may show out of session.

Summary

The purpose of the present critical analysis research study was to examine the current literature on substance abuse treatments, CBT, self-efficacy theory, self-evaluation, and self-cognition strategies to identify components of the above that are empirically important and might logically be included in a substance abuse treatment program. These components were derived from studies showing a direct relationship between longevity of treatment and successful outcomes. Self-evaluation and self-cognition are important elements in engagement in treatment.

In addition, the literature is clear that no single treatment is effective for all individuals. Treatment approaches, particularly those involving self-evaluation and self-cognition methods, were in an extensive review of the current literature to identify components that have been empirically supported and might logically be included in a substance abuse treatment program.

In this study, an intervention was developed with the goal of reducing substance abuse by helping participants become more aware of their feelings and coping reactions and changing them in ways that will support cessation of substance abuse. It is anticipated that this intervention can lead to significant changes in substance abusers' perspectives on their use of substances and on their behaviors, resulting in long-term recovery.

References

Aharonovich, E., P. C. Amrhein, A. Bisaga, E. V. Nunes, and D. S. Hasin. 2008. "Cognition, Commitment Language, and Behavioral Change among Cocaine-Dependent Patients." *Psychology of Addictive Behaviors* 22(4): 557–562.

American Psychiatric Association (APA). 2000. *Diagnostic and Statistical Manual of Mental Disorders (DSM-IV-TR)*. 4th ed. text revision. Washington, DC: Author.

Ball, S. A. 2007. "Cognitive-Behavioral and Schema-Based Models for the Treatment of Substance Abuse Disorders." In *Cognitive Schemas and Core Beliefs in Psychological Problems: A Scientist-Practitioner Guide* (pp. 111–138). Eds. In L. P. Riso, P. L. du Toit, D. J. Stein, and J. E. Young. Washington, DC, US: American Psychological Association.

Bandura, A. 1986. *Social Foundations of Thought and Action: A Social Cognitive Theory*. Englewood Cliffs, NJ: Prentice-Hall.

Bandura, A. 1997. *Self-Efficacy: The Exercise of Control*. New York: Freeman.

Beck, J. S., B. S. Liese, and L. M. Najavits. 2005. "Cognitive Therapy." In *Clinical Textbook of Addictive Disorders* (pp. 474–501). Eds. R. J. Francis, S. I. Miller, and A. Mack. New York: Guilford.

Benda, B. B. 2002. "Factors Associated with Rehospitalization among Veterans in a Substance Abuse Treatment Program." *Psychiatric Services* 53: 1176–1178.

Beck, A. T. 1975. *Cognitive Therapy and the Emotional Disorders.* Madison, CT: International Universities Press.

Beck, A. T., F. D. Wright, B.S. Liese, and C. F. Newman. 2001. *Cognitive Therapy of Substance Abuse.* New York: Guilford Press.

Beutler, L. E. 2004. "The Empirically-Supported Treatments Movement: A Scientist-Practitioner's Response." *Clinical Psychology: Science and Practice* 11: 225–229.

Carroll, K. M. 1996. "Relapse Prevention as a Psychosocial Treatment: A Review of Controlled Clinical Trials." *Experimental and Clinical Psychopharmacology* 4: 46–54.

———. 1998. *A Cognitive-Behavioral Approach: Treating Cocaine Addiction* (NIH Publication 98–4308). Rockville, MD: National Institutes on Drug Abuse.

Carroll, K. M., and L. S. Onken. 2005. "Behavioral Therapies for Drug Abuse." *American Journal of Psychiatry* 162: 1452-1460.

Carroll, K. M., B. J. Rounsaville, L. T. Gordon, C. Nich, P. Jatlow, R. M. Bisighini, et al. 1994. "Psychotherapy and Pharmacotherapy for Ambulatory Cocaine Abusers." *Archives of General Psychiatry* 51: 177–87.

Carroll, K. M., B. J. Rounsaville, C. Nich, L. T. Gordon, P. W. Wirtz, and F. H. Gawin. 1994. "One-Year Follow-Up of Psychotherapy and Pharmacotherapy for Cocaine Dependence: Delayed Emergence of Psychotherapy Effects." *Archives of General Psychiatry* 5: 989–997.

De Leon, G. 1995. "Therapeutic Communities for Addictions: A Theoretical Framework." *International Journal of the Addictions* 30: 1603–1645.

Diaz, N., E. G. Horton, J. McIlveen, M. Weiner, and Nelson. 2008. "Dysthymia among Substance Abusers: An Exploratory Study of Individual and Mental Health Factors." *International Journal of Mental Health and Addiction* 7(2): 1557-1874.

Dolan, S. L., R. A. Martin, and D. J. Rohsenow. 2008. Self-Efficacy for Cocaine Abstinence: "Pretreatment Correlates and Relationship to Outcomes." *Addictive Behaviors* 33(5): 675-688.

Drescher, J. 2008. "A History of Homosexuality and Organized Psychoanalysis." *Journal of the American Academy of Psychoanalysis and Dynamic Psychiatry* 36(3): 443-460.

Fisher, G. L., and N. A. Roget. 2008. *Encyclopedia of Substance Abuse Prevention, Treatment, and Recovery.* Thousand Oaks, CA: Sage.

Folkman, S., and J. T. Moskowitz. 2000. "Positive Affect and the Other Side of Coping." *American Psychologist* 55: 647-654.

Freud, S. 1955. "Beyond the Pleasure Principle." In *The Standard Edition of the Complete Psychological Works of Sigmund Freud* 18: 3–64. Edited and Translated by J. Strachey. London: Hogarth Press (original work published 1915)

———. 1957. "The Unconscious." In *The Standard Edition of the Complete Psychological Works of Sigmund Freud* 14: 166–204. Edited and Translated by J. Strachey. Hogarth: London (original work published in 1915)

Futterman, R., M. Lorente, and Silverman. 2005. "Beyond Harm Reduction: A New Model of Substance Abuse Treatment Further Integrating Psychological Techniques." *Journal of Psychotherapy Integration* 15(1): 3-18.

Galliher, R. V., C. M. Evans, and Weiser. 2007. "Social and Individual Predictors of Substance Use for Native American Youth." *Journal of Child and Adolescent Substance Abuse* 16(3): 1-17.

Goldfried, M. R. 2006. *A Casebook of Psychotherapy Integration*. Washington DC: American Psychiatric Association.

Guydish, J. 2003. "Introduction: Dissemination from Practice to Research." In *Drug Abuse Treatment through Collaboration: Practice and Research Partnerships that Work* (pp. 13–16). Eds. J. L. Sorensen, R. A. Rawson, J. Guydish, and J. E. Zweben. Washington, DC: American Psychological Association.

Hartel, C. R., and Glantz. 1999. The Treatment of Drug Abuse: Changing the Paths. In *Drug abuse: Origins and Interventions* (pp. 243–284). Eds. M. D. Glantz and C. R. Hartel. Washington, DC: American Psychological Association.

Hayes, S. C., K. D. Strosahl, and K. G. Wilson. 2003. *Acceptance and Commitment Therapy: An Experiential Approach to Behavior Change*. New York: Guilford.

Hopper, E. 1995. "A Psychoanalytical Theory of 'Drug Addiction': Unconscious Fantasies of Homosexuality, Compulsions, and Masturbation within the Context of Traumatogenic Processes." *International Journal of Psychoanalysis* 76: 1121-1142.

Huber, A., W. Ling, S. Shoptaw, V. Gulati, P. Brethen, and R. A. Rawson. 1997. "Integrating Treatments for Methamphetamine Abuse: A Psychosocial Approach." *Journal of Addictive Diseases* 16: 41–0.

Kaplan, H. B. 2008. "Self Theory and Emotions." In *Handbook of the Sociology of Emotions* (pp. 224-249). Eds. J. E. Stets and J. H. Turner. New York: Springer.

Koole, S. L., and L. H. Coenen. 2007. "Implicit Self and Affect Regulation: Effects of Action Orientation and Subliminal Self Priming in an Affective Priming Task." *Self and Identity* 6: 118-136.

Kranz, K. M., and O'Hare. 2006. "The Substance Abuse Treatment Self-Efficacy Scale: A Confirmatory Factor Analysis." *Journal of Social Service Research* 32(3): 109-121.

Lazarus, R. S., and S. Folkman. 1994. *Stress, Appraisal, and Coping.* New York: Springer.

Levant, R. F. 2004. "The Empirically Validated Treatments Movement: A Practitioner's Perspective." *Clinical Psychology: Science and Practice* 11: 219–224.

Levin, C., M. Ilgen, and R. Moos. 2007. "Avoidance Coping Strategies Moderate the Relationship between Self-Efficacy and 5-Year Alcohol Treatment Outcomes." *Psychology of Addictive Behaviors* 21(1): 108–113.

Litt, M. D., R. M. Kadden, E. Kabela-Cormier, and N. M. Petry. 2008. "Coping Skills Training and Contingency Management Treatments for Marijuana Dependence: Exploring Mechanisms of Behavior Change. *Addiction* 103: 638–648.

Litt, M. D, R. M. Kadden, and R. S. Stephens. 2005. "Coping and Self-Efficacy in Marijuana Treatment: Results from the Marijuana Treatment Project." *Journal of Consulting and Clinical Psychology* 73(6): 1015–1025.

Margolin, A., Z. Schuman-Olivier, M. Beitel, R. M. Arnold, C. E. Fulwiler, and S. K. Avants. 2007. "A Preliminary Study of Spiritual Self-Schema (3-S) Therapy for Reducing Impulsivity in HIV-Positive Drug Users." *Journal of Clinical Psychology* 63(10): 979–999.

Marlatt, G. A. 1985. "Relapse Prevention: Theoretical Rationale and Overview of the Model." In *Relapse Prevention* (pp. 250–280). Eds. G. A. Marlatt and J. R. Gordon. New York: Guilford Press.

———. 1996. "Models of Relapse and Relapse Prevention: A Commentary." *Experimental Clinical Psychopharmacology* 55-60.

———. Ed. 1998. *Harm Reduction: Pragmatic Strategies for Managing High-Risk Behaviors.* New York: Guilford Press.

Marlatt, G. A., and J. R. Gordon. 1985. *Relapse Prevention: Maintenance Strategies in the Treatment of Addictive Behaviors.* New York: Guilford Press.

Marlatt, G. A., A. W. Blume, and G. A. Parks. 2001. "Integrating Harm Reduction Therapy and Traditional Substance Abuse Treatment." *Journal of Psychoactive Drugs* 33(1): 13–21.

Marlatt, G. A., and D. M. Donovan. 2005. *Relapse Prevention: Maintenance Strategies in the Treatment of Addictive Behaviors.* 2nd ed. New York: Guilford.

Matto, H. M. 2007. "An Innovative Treatment: Stage I Evaluation of a Dual Processing Treatment Protocol on Self-Regulation Capacities of Chronic Substance Dependent Adults." *Best Practices in Mental Health* 3(1): 41-51.

McCusker, C. G. 2001. "Cognitive Biases and Addiction: An Evolution in Theory and Method." *Addiction* 96: 47–56.

McKellar, J., M. Ilgen, B. Moos, and R. Moos. 2008. "Predictors of Changes in Alcohol-Related Self-Efficacy over 16 Years." *Journal of Substance Abuse Treatment* 35(2): 148-155.

McLellan, A. T. 2008. "Evolution in Addiction Treatment Concepts and Methods." In *The American Psychiatric Publishing Textbook of Substance Abuse Treatment* (pp. 93-108). Eds. M. Galanter and H. D. Klerber. Arlington, VA: American Psychiatric Publishing.

Miller, P. M., and M. J. Carpenter. 2005. "Behavioral Treatments for the Addictions." *Encyclopedia of Behavior Modification and Cognitive Behavior Therapy.* Thousand Oaks, CA: SAGE Publications.

Miller, W. R., and S. Rollnick. 2002. *Motivational Interviewing.* 2nd ed. New York: Guilford Press.

Morgenstern, J. 2000. "Effective Technology Transfer in Alcoholism Treatment." *Substance Use and Misuse* 35: 1659–1678.

Nes, M. L., and T. P. S. Oei. 2005. "The Effectiveness of an Inpatient Group Cognitive Behavioral Therapy Program for Alcohol Dependence." *The American Journal on Addictions* 14: 139–154.

Otto, M. W., C. M. O'Cleirigh, and M. H. Pollack. 2007. "Attending to Emotional Cues for Drug Abuse: Bridging the Gap between Clinic and Home Behaviors." *NIDA Science and Practice Perspectives* (April): 48-55.

Ouimette, P. C., J. W. Finney, and R. H. Moos. 1997. "Twelve-Step and Cognitive-Behavioral Treatment for Substance Abuse: A Comparison of Treatment Effectiveness." *Journal of Consulting and Clinical Psychology* 65(2): 230-240.

Rawson, R. A., A. Huber, P. B. Brethen, J. L. Obert, V. Gulati, S. Shoptaw, et al. 2000. "Methamphetamine and Cocaine Users: Differences in Characteristics and Treatment Retention." *Journal of Psychoactive Drugs* 3: 233–238.

Rawson, R. A., M. J. McCann, F. Flammino, S. Shoptaw, K. Miotto, C. Rieber, et al. 2006. "A Comparison of Contingency Management and Cognitive-Behavioral Approaches for Stimulant Dependent Individuals. *Addiction* 101: 267–274.

Rawson, R. A., S. Shoptaw, J. Obert, M. McCann, A. Hasson, P. Marinelli-Casey, et al. 1995. "An Intensive Outpatient Approach for Cocaine Abuse Treatment: The Matrix Model." *Journal of Substance Abuse Treatment* 12: 117–27.

Richter, L., and P. B. Johnson. 2001. "Current Methods of Assessing Substance Use: A Review of Strengths, Problems, and Developments." *Journal of Drug Issues* 46: 34–42.

Robinson, S. I., M. Ashworth, M. Shepherd, and C. Evans. 2006. In their own words: a narrative-based classification of clients' problems on an idiographic outcome measure for talking therapy in primary care. *Primary Care Mental Health* 4: 165–73.

Rogers, C. R. 1959. *Client-Centered Therapy: Its Current Practice, Implications, and Theory.* Boston, MA: Houghton-Mifflin.

Rosay, A. B., S. S. Najaka, and D. C. Herz. 2007. "Differences in the Validity of Self-Reported Drug Use across Five Factors: Gender, Race, Age, Type of Drug, and Offense Seriousness." *Journal of Quantitative Criminology* 23: 41–58.

Rosenblum A., C. Cleland, S. Magura, D. Mahmood, and N. Kosanke. 2005. "Moderators of Effects of Motivational Enhancements to Cognitive Behavioral Therapy." *The American Journal of Drug and Alcohol Abuse* 31(1): 35–58.

Rotgers, F., J. Morgenstern, and S. T. Walters. 2006. *Treating Substance Abuse.* New York: Guilford Press.

Rudman, L. A., and S. J. Spencer. 2007. "The Implicit Self." *Self and Identity* 6: 97-100.

Shadel, W. G., and D. Cervone. 2006. "Evaluating Social–Cognitive Mechanisms that Regulate Self-Efficacy in Response to Provocative Smoking Cues: An Experimental Investigation." *Psychology of Addictive Behaviors* 20(1): 91–96.

Shoal, G. D., and P. R. Giancola. 2005. "The Relation between Social Problems and Substance Use in Adolescent Boys: An Investigation of Potential Moderators." *Experimental Clinical Psychopharmacology* 13(4): 357–66.

Shoptaw, S., R. A. Rawson, M. McCann, and J. L. Obert. 1994. "The Matrix Model of Outpatient Stimulant Abuse Treatment: Evidence of Efficacy." *Journal of Addictive Diseases* 13: 129–141.

Shoptaw, S., C. J. Reback, J. A. Peck, X. Yang, E. Rotheram-Fuller, S. Larkins, et al. 2005. Behavioral Treatment Approaches for Methamphetamine Dependence and HIV-Related Sexual Risk

Behaviors among Urban Gay and Bisexual Men. *Drug and Alcohol Dependence* 78(2): 125-134.

Sloan, J. J., M. R. Bodapati, and T. A. Tucker. 2004. "Respondent Misreporting of Drug Use in Self-Reports: Social Desirability and Other Correlates." *Journal of Drug Issues* 34: 269–292.

Stasiewicz, P. R., P. C. Vincent, C. M. Bradizza, G. J. Connors, S. A. Maisto, and N. D. Mercer. 2008. "Factors Affecting Agreement between Severely Mentally Ill Alcohol Abusers' and Collaterals' Reports of Alcohol and Other Substance Abuse." *Psychology of Addictive Behaviors* 22(1): 78-87.

Substance Abuse and Mental Health Services Administration (SAMSHA). 2003. *Traditional therapies*. Retrieved November 18, 2009. http://mentalhealth.samhsa.gov/publications/allpubs/ken98-0053/default.asp#cog_behavioral.

Tate, S. R., J. R. McQuaid, C. Shriver, M. Krenek, J. Wu, K. Cumins, et al. 2008. "Comorbidity of Substance Dependence and Depression: Role of Life Stress and Self-Efficacy in Sustaining Abstinence." *Psychology of Addictive Behaviors* 22(1): 47–57.

Tolli, A. P., A. M. Schmidt. 2008. "The Role of Feedback, Casual Attributions, and Self-Efficacy in Goal Revision." *Journal of Applied Psychology* 93: 692-701.

Twohig, M. P., and K. A. Peterson. 2008. "Distress Tolerance. In *General Principles and Empirically Supported Techniques of Cognitive Behavioral Therapy*. Eds. W. T. O'Donohue and J. E. Fisher. New York: Wiley.

Wechsberg, W. M., W. A. Zule, K. S. Riehman, W. K. Luseno, and W. K. K. Lam. 2007. "African-American Crack Abusers and Drug Treatment Initiation: Barriers and Effects of a Pretreatment Intervention." *Substance Abuse Treatment, Prevention, and Policy* 2(10). Retrieved November 18, 2009. http://www.substanceabusepolicy.com/content/2/1/10.

West, R., and A. Hardy. 2006. *Theory of Addiction*. New York: Wiley.

White, W. L. 1998. *Slaying the Dragon: The History of Addiction Treatment and Recovery in America*. Bloomington, IL: Lighthouse Training Institute.

Witkiewitz, K., and G. A. Marlatt. 2004. "Relapse Prevention for Alcohol and Drug Problems: That Was Zen, This is Tao." *American Psychologist* 59: 224–235.

———. 2007. *Therapist's Guide to Evidence-Based Relapse Prevention*. Burlington, MA: Academic Press.

Wong, E. C., and E. Longshore. 2008. "Ethnic Identity, Spirituality, and Self-Efficacy Influences on Treatment Outcomes among Hispanic American Methadone Maintenance Clients. *Journal of Ethnicity in Substance Abuse* 7(3): 328-340.

About the Author

Roham Ghassemi, has always been interested in bringing study of human cognition and psychology closer from philosophical and religious aspects. He has been studying the works by important world thinkers and the wise about cognition and self knowledge to be able to expand and contribute the relationship between physical and metaphysics levels of each individual.

Index